Created and manufactured by arrangement with Ottenheimer Publishers, Inc.
Copyright © 1991 Ottenheimer Publishers, Inc.
All rights reserved. Printed in Singapore.

My First Word Book

P.S.I. & Associates, Inc.
13322 S.W. 128th Street
Miami, Florida 33186
(305) 255-7959

The Home

light switch

picture

ceiling fan

tissues

dresser

lamp

nightstand

bedspread

bed

window

stairs

drapes

couch

television

closet

chair

rug

coatrack

lawn mower

shower curtain

shower

watering can

mirror

toilet

deck

bathtub

clock

telephone

cookie jar

refrigerator

sink

vanity

pot

cups

door

plates

cupboards

doorbell

stove

table and chairs

dryer

hot water heater

bush

washer

laundry basket

The Farm

hills

haystacks

field

farmhouse

pond

ducks

road

tractor

apples

plow

hen house

nest and eggs

chickens

squash

well

tomatoes

hoe

basket

path

goat

hutch

rabbit

The Seashore

lighthouse

sailboat

water skier

power boat

cliff

air mattress

driftwood

fish

splash

lobster

sand

innertube

seashells

seaweed

beach robe

deck chair

sandcastle

boardwalk

The Carnival

pennants

bumper cars

games of chance

merry-go-round

ticket counter

peanuts

ferris wheel

TICKETS

The Birthday Party

balloons

streamers

pin-the-tail-on-the-donkey game

blindfold

presents

ball

punch

party favors

spoons

candle

noisemaker

ice cream

birthday cake

candy

banner

HAPPY BIRTHDAY!

wand

magic show

magician

magic box

party hat

applause

coins

handkerchief

cards

audience

envelope

birthday card

The Park

monkey bars

trees

slide

friends

lake

whee!

seesaw

pipe

grass

jogger

jumprope

sandbox

swing

kite

tennis ball

tennis court

bicycle

bench

roller
skates

bee

ants

picnic

picnic
basket

cooler

picnic blanket

butterfly

fountain

flowers

Bedtime

My First Words

air mattress
ambulance
ants
apartments
applause
apples
audience
awning
ball
balloons
banner
barker
barn
basket
bathing suit
bathmat
bathrobe
bathtub
beach bag
beach ball
beach blanket
beach robe
beach shoes
beach umbrella
bearded lady
bed
bedspread
bee
bench
bicycle
birthday cake
birthday card
blanket
blindfold
boardwalk
book
bridge
bubbles
bucket
bumper cars
buoy
bus
bush
butterfly
candle
candy
car
cards
carrots
ceiling fan
chair
chickens
church

cliff
clock
closet
clouds
coatrack
coins
construction workers
cookie jar
cooler
cornfield
cotton candy
couch
cow
crab
crow
cupboards
cups
deck
deck chair
door
doorbell
drapes
dresser
driftwood
dryer
ducks
envelope
factory
farmhouse
faucet
fence
ferris wheel
field
fire escape
fire truck
fish
flippers
flowers
fountain
French fries
friends
games of chance
garden
gas station
gate
goat
grass
grocery store
hamburgers
handkerchief
hayloft
haystacks
hen house

hills
hoe
horse
hot dogs
hot water heater
hotel
hutch
ice cream
innertube
jogger
juggler
jumprope
kite
lake
lamp
laundry basket
lawn mower
lettuce
library
lifeguard
light switch
lighthouse
lobster
magic box
magic show
magician
mailbox
manhole
meadow
merry-go-round
milk can
mirror
monkey bars
movie
neighbors
nest and eggs
nighlight
nightstand
noisemaker
ocean
office
orchard
pajamas
parking lot
parking meter
party favors
party hat
path
peanuts
pennants
picnic
picnic basket
picnic blanket

picture
pier
pig
pigsty
pillow
pin-the-tail-on-
   the-donkey game
pipe
pitchfork
pizza
plates
plow
police car
pond
poster
pot
power boat
presents
punch
rabbit
rake
refrigerator
restaurant
road
roller coaster
roller skates
roof
rooster
rope
rubber duck
rug
sailboat
sand
sandbox
sandcastle
scarecrow
school
seagull
seashells
seaweed
seesaw
sheep
sheet
shore
shovel
shower
shower curtain
side show
silo
sink
skyscrapers
slide
slippers

soap
soda
splash
spoons
squash
stairs
stall
starfish
stop sign
store
stove
streamers
street
strong man
subway entrance
sun
sunglasses
sunhat
swing
table and chairs
taxicab
teddy bear
telephone
television
tennis ball
tennis court
tent
ticket counter
tissues
toilet
tomatoes
toothbrush
toothpaste
towel
toy boat
tractor
traffic light
trash can
trees
truck
vanity
vendor
wall
wand
washcloth
washer
water skier
watering can
waves
weather vane
well
whee!
window